The *History of the Alphabet*
from Egyptian to Modern Day Cursive
is dedicated to my
28th Godchild, Ryan John Jensen

I would like to give credit to Jessica Fontes
for her technical help, and to Jayne Flaagan
for her work in editing and publishing this work.

Theresa Wald

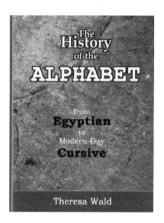

Husky Publishing
East Grand Forks, MN
Copyright © 2016 Theresa Wald
Cover Design copyright © Jayne Flaagan

Emergence of the Cursive Alphabet

The history of writing began with the first crude pictures of wild animals on the walls, caves and rock shelters. About the same time, the Sumerians invented a system of writing that used wedge-shaped symbols.

There were three great steps in the development of a full alphabet. The first step was taken in the years around 900 B.C. by the Sumerians. The second step was credited to the Semitic society. The third step of the alphabet was created by the Greeks. These three stages of development involved *word, syllabic* and *alphabetic*.

Both manuscript and cursive alphabets came from the Roman alphabet. Manuscript is the style most frequently used in teaching. It started in Great Britain and the United States about 1900.

The word *cursive* means *running*. In cursive, the letters join, or run together, instead of being separated, as in manuscript writing. The letters in cursive are slanted.

Here is an example of cursive writing:

a b c d e f g

When a right-handed person writes cursive, the paper is slanted to the left. For left- handed people, the paper slants to the right.

Children learn the most about cursive writing by watching a teacher write well. Mastering cursive writing is often seen by children as a rite of passage. It's the kind of writing grown-ups do. It is suggested that children be taught cursive writing at age seven, about second grade. Cursive is usually learned after boys and girls have mastered manuscript writing.

It is common to pick up a pencil and start writing cursive. Handwriting in the cursive mode remains an important skill in modern living. However, technology has developed rapidly over the recent years and cursive is being used less and less.

When children can automatically write each letter without having to labor over it too much, their minds are freed up for higher-level thinking; children will read with more fluency. They will also write faster because their mental energy can be devoted to expressing their thoughts on paper, rather than on forming each individual letter correctly.
A child needs a strong sense of left and right. Cursive can help with that too.

Personalization is another positive asset of cursive writing. When you read someone's cursive writing, you are receiving a piece of that writer's personality.

If cursive disappears, how will people sign their name in any distinctive manner that makes one person's handwriting different from another person's handwriting?

Being able to write in cursive can even be critical at certain times. For example, in an emergency situation, one can write in cursive faster than one can write in print.

There are many reasons we need to continue to teach our young children how to write in cursive. If we do not, we will be taking a step backward in the English language.

Cursive writing is still very essential in this modern age. It needs to be preserved.

Contents

A a

Egyptians		The ancient Egyptians, about 3000 B.C., drew the symbol of an ox's head.
Semites		The Semites simplified the Egyptian symbol about 1500 B.C. They called their letter "*aelph,*" their word for "*ox.*"
Phoenician		About 1000 B.C. the Phoenicians simplified the semitic letter.
Greeks		The Greeks adapted the letter about 600 B.C. They called their letter "*alpha*" and made it the first letter of their alphabet.
Romans		The Romans gave the letter **A** its present form about A.D. 114.
Cursive		**A** is about the third most frequently used letter.

B b

Egyptians

The ancient Egyptian, about 3000 B.C. , drew the symbol of house.

Semites

The Semites modified the Egyptian symbol about 1500 B.C. They called the letter "*beth*," the word for "*house.*"

Phoenician

About 1000 B.C. the Phoenicians drew the symbol of a house and a doorway.

Greeks

The Greeks changed the Phoenician symbol and added it to their alphabet around 600 B.C. They called the letter *"beta."*

Romans

The Romans rounded the **B** to its present form about A.D. 114.

Cursive

B is about the 20th most frequently used letter.

C c

Egyptians		The ancient Egyptians, about 3000 B.C., wrote a symbol that represented a boomerang. The letters **C** and **G** both developed from this symbol.
Phoenicians		The Phoenicians, about 1000 B.C., used a symbol that looked like a book.
Greeks		The Greeks wrote the letter as a right angle about 600 B.C. They made it their third letter and called it "*gamma*."
Romans	C	The Romans, about A.D. 114, gave the letter **C** the curved form it has today.
Cursive		**C** is about the 13th most frequently used letter.

D d

Egyptians

The ancient Egyptians drew the symbol of a door with panels about 3000 B.C. The Semites adopted the symbol and named it *"daleth,"* their name for *door*.

Phoenician

The Phoenicians used a triangle in their alphabet about 1000 B.C.

Greeks

The Greeks, about 600 B.C., shaped their letter as an equilateral triangle. They called their letter *"delta."*

Romans

D

The Romans rounded the letter and gave it its capital form about A.D. 114.

Cursive

The letter **D** is about the 10th most frequently used letter.

E e

Egyptians		The ancient Egyptian, about 3000 B.C., wrote a symbol that represented a person shouting with joy.
Semites		The Semites, about 1500 B.C. , used a letter they called the "*He*." They drew it as a figure of someone shouting.
Phoenicians		The Phoenicians included this simple figure in their alphabet around 1000 B.C.
Greeks		The Greeks changed the letter and added it to their alphabet about 600 B.C. They named the letter "*epsilon*."
Romans		The Romans gave the letter **E** its present form about A.D. 114.
Cursive		**E** is the most frequently used letter.

F f

Egyptians/ Semites	Y	The ancient Egyptian drew this symbol of a hook about 3000 B.C. The Semites adopted the symbol and named it *"waw,"* their word for *hook*.
Phoenicians	Y	The Phoenicians used this symbol of a hook in their alphabet about 1000 B.C.
Greeks	F	The Greeks, about 800 B.C., changed the symbol and made it the sixth letter of their alphabet. They called it *"digamma."*
Romans	F	The Romans gave the capital **F** its present form about A.D. 114.
Cursive	F f	**F** is about the 15th most frequently used letter.

G g

Egyptians

The ancient Egyptian, about 3,000 B.C., wrote a symbol that represented a boomerang. The letters **C** and **G** both developed from this symbol.

Phoenicians

The Phoenicians, about 1000 B.C., used a symbol that looked like a hook.

Greeks

The Greeks wrote the letter as a right angle about 600 B.C. They made it their third letter and called it "*gamma*."

Romans

The Romans gave the letter **G** its final form about A.D. 114.

Cursive

G is about the 18th most frequently used letter.

H h

Egyptians

The ancient Egyptians, about 3000 B.C., wrote a symbol that represented a twisted length of rope.

Semites

The Semites modified the Egyptian symbol about 1500 B.C. They called it *"cheth."*

Phoenician

The Phoenicians, about 1000 B.C., made the letter with three cross bars.

Greeks

The Greeks added the letter to their alphabet about 600 B.C. They named the letter *"eta."*

Romans

The Romans borrowed the letter from the Greeks about A.D. 114. They gave the **H** the shape and sound it has today.

Cursive

H is the ninth most frequently used letter.

I i

Egyptians

The ancient Egyptians drew this symbol of a hand about 3000 B.C.

Semites

The Semites modified the symbol for their alphabet about 1500 B.C.

Phoenician

The Phoenicians changed the Semite letter about 1000 B.C. They named it "*yod*," which was their word for *hand*.

Greeks

The Greeks, about 600 B.C., made the letter a single stroke called "*iots*."

Romans

The Romans gave the letter **I** its present shape about A.D. 114.

Cursive

I is the seventh most frequently used letter.

J j

Egyptians		The ancient Egyptians drew this symbol of a hand about 3000 B.C. The letters **J** and **I** developed from this symbol.
Semites		The Semites simplified the symbol for their alphabet about 1500 B.C.
Phoenicians		The Phoenicians changed the Semite letter about 1000 B.C. They named it "*yod*," which was the word for *hand.*
Greeks		The Greeks, about 600 B.C., made the letter a single stroke called "*iots.*"
Romans		The Romans gave the letter **J** its present shape about A.D. 114.
Medieval		The medieval scribes added a tail to the **J** when it appeared in certain positions. The **J** developed from this practice.
Cursive		**J** is the 24th most frequently used letter.

K k

Egyptians

The ancient Egyptians, about 3000 B.C.,used a symbol that represented a slightly cupped hand.

Semites

The Semites simplified the symbol for their alphabet about 1500 B.C. They named the letter "*kaph*," which was their word for *hand*.

Phoenician

The Phoenicians wrote the letter with three prongs about 1000 B.C.

Greeks

The Greeks, about 600 B.C., gave the letter the form that is used today. They called the letter "*kappa*."

Romans

The Romans adopted the Greek letter about A.D. 114.

Cursive

K is the 22nd most frequently used letter.

L l

Egyptians		The ancient Egyptians, about 3000 B.C., used a symbol that represented a crooked staff called a "*goad*."
Semites		The Semites adopted the Egyptian symbol about 1500 B.C. They named the letter "*lamed*," which was their word for "*goad.*"
Phoenician		The Phoenicians used a symbol of an upside down staff about 1000 B.C.
Greeks		The Greeks added the letter to their alphabet about 600 B.C. They called it "*lambda*."
Romans	L	The Romans gave the letter **L** its present shape about A.D. 114.
Cursive		**L** is the 11th most frequently used letter.

M m

Egyptians		The ancient Egyptians, about 3000 B.C.,drew this symbol of waves of water.
Semites		The Semites adopted the Egyptian symbol about 1500 B.C. They named the letter "*mem*," which was their word for *water*.
Phoenician		The Phoenicians changed the Semite letter about 1000 B.C.
Greeks		The Greeks added the letter "*mu*" to their alphabet about 600 B.C.
Romans		The Romans, about A.D. 114, gave the **M** its capital shape.
Cursive		**M** is the 14th most frequently used letter.

N n

Egyptians		The ancient Egyptians drew this symbol of a snake about 3000 B.C.
Semites		The Semites, about 1500 B.C., wrote the letter in this form.
Phoenician		The Phoenicians simplified the Semitic symbol about 1000 B.C.
Greeks	**N**	The Greeks changed the letter and added it to their alphabet about 600 B.C. They called it "*nu*."
Romans	**N**	The Romans, about A.D. 114, wrote the letter **N** with straight lines.
Cursive		**N** is the fifth most frequently used letter.

O o

Egyptians

The ancient Egyptians drew this symbol of an eye about 3000 B.C.

Semites

The Semites simplified the Egyptian symbol about 1500 B.C. They named the letter "*ayin*," their word for *eye*.

Phoenician

The Phoenicians, about 1000 B.C., drew the letter as a circle.

Greeks

The Greeks borrowed the letter from the Phoenicians about 600 B.C. The Greek letter was called "*omicron.*"

Romans

The Romans, about A.D. 114, gave the letter **O** its graceful shape.

Cursive

O is the fourth most frequently used letter.

P p

Egyptians

The ancient Egyptians used this symbol for *mouth*, about 3000 B.C.

Semites

The Semites, about 1500 B.C., adopted the Egyptian symbol. They used it for the letter "*pe*," their word for "*mouth*."

Phoenician

The Phoenicians used a rounded hook-shaped letter about 1000 B.C.

Greeks

The Greeks squared the hook and added it to their alphabet around 600 B.C .

Romans

The Romans gave the **P** its present shape about A.D. 114.

Cursive

P is the 18th most frequently used letter.

Q q

Egyptians		The ancient Egyptians, about 3000 B.C., drew a symbol of a monkey
Semites		The Semites adopted the symbol and named it "*goph*," the word for *ape* or *monkey*.
Phoenicians		The Phoenicians used a symbol of a knotted cord to write the letter "*goph*" about 1500 B.C.
Greeks		The Greeks, about 800 B.C., developed a G-shaped letter called '*koppa*." This letter was seldom used.
Romans		The Romans gave the **Q** its present form about A.D. 114.
Cursive		**Q** is the 25th most frequently used letter.

R r

Egyptians

The ancient Egyptians, about 3000 B.C., wrote a symbol of a human head.

Semites

The Semites adopted the Egyptian symbol about 1500 B.C. They called the letter "*resh*," the word for *head*.

Phoenicians

The Phoenicians, about 1000 B.C., changed the Semitic symbol and made it a triangle with a tail.

Greeks

The Greeks used the P-shaped letter about 600 B.C. They called it "*rho*."

Romans

The Romans gave the **R** its capital form about A.D. 114.

Cursive

R is the sixth most frequently used letter.

S s

Egyptians		The ancient Egyptians drew this symbol of a tusk about 3000 B.C.
Semites		The Semites, about 1500 BC., developed a letter called "*shin*," which was their word for *tooth*.
Phoenician	W	The Phoenicians squared off the letter about 1000 B.C.
Greeks	Σ	The Greeks, about 600 B.C., turned the letter on its side and called it "*sigma*."
Romans	S	The Romans gave the **S** its capital form about A.D. 114.
Cursive		**S** is the eighth most frequently used letter.

T t

Egyptians	X	The ancient Egyptians used this check mark about 3000 B.C.
Semites	+	The Semites, about 1500 B.C. used a cross-shaped letter. They called it "*taw*, their word for *mark*.
Phoenician	+	The Phoenicians had a cross-shaped letter in their alphabet about 1000 B.C.
Greeks	T	The Greeks, about 600 B.C., put the cross bar at the top of the vertical stroke. They called the letter "*tau*."
Romans	T	The Romans gave the **T** its capital form about A.D. 114.
Cursive	*T t*	**T** is the second most frequently used letter.

U u

Egyptians	Y	The ancient Egyptians drew this symbol of a supporting pole about 3000 B.C.
Semites	Y	The Semites adopted the symbol and named it "*waw*," their word for *hook*.
Phoenician	Y	The Phoenicians made a letter like a hook about 1000 B.C.
Greeks	T	The Greeks added the letter *upsilon* to their alphabet about 600 B.C.
Romans	V	The Romans used the letter **V** for both the **U** and the **V** sound about A.D. 114.
Medieval	U	The Medieval scholars began writing **U** for a vowel and **V** for a consonant.
Cursive	*U u*	**U** is the 12th most frequently used letter.

V v

Egyptians	Y	The ancient Egyptians drew this symbol of a supporting pole about 3000 B.C.
Semites	Y	The Semites adopted the symbol and called it "*waw*," their word for *hook*.
Phoenician	Y	The Phoenicians used this symbol of a hook in their alphabet about 1000 B.C.
Greeks	T	The Greeks changed the symbol about 600 B.C. They called their letter "*upsilon*."
Romans	V	The Romans gave the **V** its capital form about A.D. 114.
Cursive	*V v*	**V** is the 21st most frequently used letter.

W w

Egyptians	Y	The ancient Egyptians drew this symbol of a supporting pole about 3000 B.C.
Semites	Y	The Semites adopted the symbol and named it "*waw*," their word for *hook*.
Phoenician	Y	The Phoenicians used this symbol of a hook in their alphabet about 1000 B.C.
Greeks	T	The Greeks changed the symbol and added it to their alphabet about 600 B.C. They called it "*upsilon*."
Romans	V	The Romans gave the letter **V** its present shape about A.D. 114.
Medieval	W	The medieval scribes used **VV** as a letter about 1000. **W** was also written **UU** and the letter became known as "*double U*."
Cursive	*W w*	**W** is the 19th most frequently used letter.

X x

Phoenicians

The Phoenicians developed this symbol for the letter "*samekh*," about 1000 B.C.

Greeks

The Greeks changed the symbol about 600 B.C. They called the letter "*chi*."

Romans

The Romans, about A.D. 114, gave the letter **X** its final capital form.

Cu rsive

X is the 23rd most commonly used letter.

Y y

Egyptians

The ancient Egyptians drew this symbol of a supporting pole about 3000 B.C.

Semites

The Semites adopted the symbol and named it "*waw*," their word for *hook*.

Phoenician

The Phoenicians used this symbol of a hook in their alphabet about 1000 B.C.

Greeks

The Greeks changed the letter and added it to their alphabet about 600 B.C. They called it "*upsilon.*"

Romans

The Romans used the letter Z when they wrote words borrowed from Greece about A.D. 114.

Cursive

Y is the 17th most frequently used letter.

31

Z z

Egyptians		The ancient Egyptians drew this symbol of an arrow about 3000 B.C.
Semites		The Semites simplified the Egyptian symbol about 1500 B.C. They named the letter "zayin," their word for weapon.
Phoenician		The Phoenicians used this symbol of a weapon about 1000 B.C.
Greeks		The Greeks changed the symbol, about 600 B.C., and made it the sixth letter of their alphabet. They called it "*zeta*."
Romans		The Romans used the letter Z when they wrote words borrowed from the Greeks about A.D. 114.
Cursive		**Z** is the least used letter.

About the Author

Theresa Wald was raised in a home where both parents were present. She attended a one- room elementary school, where her father was on the school board.

During WWII, Wald helped build the *Navy Wild Cat* plane at Eastern Aircraft in Linden N.J., where she was awarded the Army-Navy "*E*," for excellent performance during war time.

Wald received a Bachelor's degree from Minot State University in North Dakota and has credits from eight other institutions of higher learning, including universities in North Dakota, Minnesota, and Canada. Her focus of studies has been in the field of business, an area she has predominately worked in throughout her adult life.

The author has traveled to eight different countries, visiting some of the countries several times. She enjoys writing, painting, sewing, reading, weaving and painting. Wald's oil and acrylic paintings have been displayed at two art shows, one of them at *Lowe's Gardens*. However, due to failing vision, the author no longer paints.

Wald is a member of the *Order Franciscans Secular* religious group and writes a column for that organization. She was recently awarded the *Silver Star* pin by the American Legion Auxiliary for loss of a loved one.

Theresa Wald has had poems published in *Prairie People's Magazine, Plainswoman, Inner Reflections, A College Poetry Anthology, Editor's Choice Series,* and *the International Library of Poetry.* "***The History of Writing***" is Theresa Wald's sixth published book.

The author has lived on both the east and west coast. She currently resides in Grand Forks, ND

This book is available for purchase at www.amazon.com

If you have any comments or questions regarding this publication, please contact Husky Publishing at: djflaagan@gra.midco.net

18560990R00023

Printed in Great Britain
by Amazon